OUR WALK

REFLECTIONS ON THE EARLY CHURCH

KENNETH SCHENCK

Copyright © 2015 by Kenneth Schenck
Published by Wesleyan Publishing House
Indianapolis, Indiana 46250
Printed in the United States of America
ISBN: 978-0-89827-939-9
ISBN (e-book): 978-0-89827-940-5

Library of Congress Cataloging-in-Publication Data

Schenck, Kenneth, 1966-
 Our walk / Kenneth Schenck.
   pages cm
 ISBN 978-0-89827-939-9 (pbk.)
 1. Bible. James--Meditations. I. Title.
 BS2785.54.S34 2015
 227'.9106--dc23
                                  2015002102

All Scripture quotations, unless otherwise indicated, are taken from the Holy Bible, New International Version®, NIV ®. Copyright ©1973, 1978, 1984, 2011 by Biblica, Inc. Used by permission of Zondervan. All rights reserved worldwide. www.zondervan.com. The "NIV" and "New International Version" are trademarks registered in the United States Patent and Trademark Office by Biblica, Inc.

All rights reserved. No part of this publication may be reproduced, stored in a retrieval system, or transmitted in any form or by any means—electronic, mechanical, photocopy, recording, or any other—except for brief quotations in printed reviews, without the prior written permission of the publisher.

CONTENTS

Introduction	5
Week 1. Enduring Trials	9
Week 2. Doers of the Word	26
Week 3. Faith and Works	43
Week 4. Taming the Tongue	60
Week 5. God's Friends	77
Week 6. The Lord Is Coming!	94

For free shepherding resources, visit
www.wphresources.com/ourwalk.

INTRODUCTION

The book of James is a collection of wisdom that we traditionally associate with the James who was the leader of the church of Jerusalem. Paul called him "the Lord's brother" in Galatians 1:19, so he was likely the same James mentioned in Matthew 13:55. Jesus' mother and brothers did not fully understand Jesus' mission while he was on earth, but they came to believe Jesus was the Messiah after his death and resurrection. James would go on to become the leader of the Christian community in Jerusalem.

Since the churches of Jerusalem likely met in houses, there were, no doubt, many of them, and they would have been overwhelmingly, if not entirely, Jewish. The conflict in Acts 6 suggests that James was primarily connected with the house churches where Aramaic was spoken, which was probably the majority of them. Following the general pattern of Jerusalem leadership, the Jerusalem community of believers was probably guided by a council of elders (Acts 15:4; 21:18), over which James likely presided.

James died around the year AD 62. In between Roman governors, the high priest of Jerusalem had him put to death. This fact suggests that the high priest saw him as a threat in some way but did not want to confront him through the Roman system. With a Roman governor present, he would have had to obtain permission to have someone put to death.

While it is possible to outline the book of James, it is not a letter quite like Paul's letters. It is rather a collection of wisdom on themes like trials and temptations, the need to put personal faith into action, the importance of controlling the tongue, and the need to rely on God rather than worldly wealth. A couple verses capture most of the teaching of this collection.

One is James 1:19: "My dear brothers and sisters, take note of this: Everyone should be quick to listen, slow to speak and slow to become angry." Another is James 1:17: "Every good and perfect gift is from above, coming down from the Father of the heavenly lights, who does not change like shifting shadows." While it is tempting to rely on the easy way to find a source for our needs—which in James' day was the rich patron—we should rely on God. God is the one who gives every good and perfect gift. By contrast, "friendship with the world means enmity against God" (James 4:4).

This book presents six weeks of Bible studies that walk through the book of James in the New Testament. Each individual week has five devotionals, looking at a number of verses each day. The aim is to experience life transformation by hearing God speak to us through the words he revealed to the audience of James in the first century of the church. We want to hear God speak to us through Scripture and then live faithfully to his Word through the power of the Holy Spirit.

Week 1

ENDURING TRIALS
James 1:1–18

Blessed is the one who perseveres under
trial because, having stood the test, that person
will receive the crown of life that the Lord
has promised to those who love him.

—JAMES 1:12

Day 1
JOYFUL TRIALS
James 1:1-4

INTRODUCTION

After more or less greeting Christians everywhere, James gave his first bit of wisdom "to the twelve tribes scattered among the nations" (James 1:1). Trials may be difficult, but God can use them to help us grow.

ENGAGE

James was written "to the twelve tribes." At first glance, we might think he was just writing to Jews who were scattered throughout the world. But he was surely writing specifically to believers, not to all Jews. Most Jews did not believe Jesus was the Messiah at this time. We can also wonder if James also included in this group those Gentiles (or non-Jews) who believed as well. There is nothing distinctly Jewish about James, which may hint in this direction. However, even though James 1:1 may address the whole world, some passages in the book of James feel like they belong more to the agricultural world of Palestine, for example, its comments about harvesters (5:4).

The only way to learn strong faith is to endure great trials.

—GEORGE MÜELLER

EXAMINE

We find hints of the kinds of trials believers were facing in the first century in the rest of James' letter. For example, in 2:6, James mentioned that the Christians in his audience found themselves exploited by the wealthy around them. We can infer that his audience did not have an abundance of resources and often found themselves at the mercy of those who might pay them for their work. James 5:4 suggests that such landowners sometimes cheated their workers. There is perhaps even a hint in 5:6 that James especially had in mind the wealthy leadership of Jerusalem, people like the priests who had Jesus put to death. James encouraged his audience to develop endurance. Christ will end the suffering soon enough.

EXPLORE

Some people have a knack at seeing the silver lining to unpleasant things. Perhaps it is taking it too far to say there is a silver lining in all of our trials. But God regularly uses our trials and sufferings to make us into more mature people of greater character. True, we can become bitter after a trial. Some turn away from God in a crisis, like a person who tries to run a race without having done the training to prepare. But if we will let him, God can use a trial to deepen our trust in him. A trial can make us better appreciate what we have from God. Even more, we are able to help others when they face trials.

PRAYER

Father, prepare us for the time of trial. Then when it comes, sustain us through the power of your Spirit.

Day 2
ASKING FOR WISDOM
James 1:5-8

INTRODUCTION

In the context of enduring trials, James told his audience that God is someone who wants to give them wisdom. But they should only ask if they really want it.

ENGAGE

God wants to give us wisdom at all times. However, the context here is when we are facing trials. Therefore, James was probably talking about how eager God is to give us wisdom when we are facing a trial. God not only wants to give us the wisdom to endure the trial; he is eager to give us that wisdom. He will be generous with it. He will show us how to make it through. He only insists that we are completely serious about wanting his wisdom. The worst would be for someone to ask for and receive wisdom, only to throw it away. God has no interest in giving wisdom to this type of person. That person will receive nothing of the sort.

*If, then a man in truth wills the Good,
then he must be willing to do all for it or he
must be willing to suffer all for it.*

—SØREN KIERKEGAARD

EXAMINE

James' warning to the "double-minded" (v. 7) person who doubts has probably brought fear to some people with an overactive conscience. This sensitive soul is prone to mistake passing thoughts for the kinds of doubts James had in mind. But James was not thinking of a mere thought, even a doubt, that might run through your head. James was thinking of a double-minded person as someone with divided loyalties. This is the person who is not sure that he or she really wants to stay with God through the time of trial. This person might go with God in the good times but take the easy way out in hard times. It is this person, whose *choices* waver, that James had in mind.

EXPLORE

It is easy for us to think that we can live the Christian life without asking others—let alone God—for help. How many people try to weather the storms of life without utilizing God's wisdom? God is not some twisted torturer who enjoys watching us suffer. He wants to help us. On the one hand, he knows that trials can be good for our faith. They can build our endurance. They can strengthen our faith and our resolve to follow the Lord. But just because God allows us to go through the storms does not mean he does not want to help us through. Like a good teacher, he wants to teach us how to endure. We only need ask for his instruction.

PRAYER

Father, give us the wisdom to keep taking the next step or to stand in place as the hurricanes of life blow against us.

Day 3
PROUD HUMILITY
James 1:9–12

INTRODUCTION

These verses follow James' encouragement for Christians to ask for wisdom when they are facing trials. They suggest that James especially had in mind the person in humble circumstances.

ENGAGE

Assuming that James was not just throwing out individual pearls of wisdom, these few verses probably tell us whom James had been picturing all along. What type of person did he have in mind as he encouraged Christians to endure trials with joy? Apparently, he especially had in mind the person in humble circumstances. His words to them remind us of what Jesus said in the Beatitudes:

"Blessed are the poor in spirit, for theirs is the kingdom of heaven" (Matt. 5:3). Those of little means may be nothing in the eyes of the world, but in God's eyes, they have a high position, especially if they are part of the people of God.

It is easier for a camel to go through the eye of a needle than for someone who is rich to enter the kingdom of God.

—Mark 10:25

EXAMINE

James had nothing positive to say about those with wealth in his day. When he spoke of the wealthy, he may have had the leaders of Jerusalem, especially its wealthy Sadducean priests, in mind (for example, James 5:6). Here he said that the proud, rich person will wither away. Such individuals will pass away like wildflowers. Their blossoms will fall. James had no time for people who go around with money-making projects, greedy to amass things for themselves. He said those people will fade away even while off on business. What is so important to those people will suddenly be revealed as trivial. The eternal will burst into the eternally insignificant.

EXPLORE

Because you are reading this devotional, it is likely that you are rich compared to the Christians of the first century. But we do not live in the same economic world that James did. The average person can get a job that, if he or she is wise with the money, can bring a standard of living far above that of the first century. Yet most of us are probably too quick to let ourselves off the hook. We do not feel the inner tension we should when we read passages like this. Once we have enough money to live on, our next thought should be how to help others with our excess.

PRAYER

Spirit, grab hold of our attention to see the eternal—now and not just when it forces its way into our thinking.

Day 4

DON'T BLAME GOD
James 1:13–15

INTRODUCTION

In these verses, James quickly corrected those who would say that God, let alone the Devil, made them do something wrong. God is not in the business of trying to get us to fail. The responsibility lies with us.

ENGAGE

James 1:13 is a very important verse in the Bible. It tells us that God is not in the business of tempting people. God doesn't try to get us to fail, and he doesn't get a certain fiendish delight when we do. God wants us to succeed when we face trials and are tempted to find the wrong way out. There are certainly stories in the Old Testament that sound like God was tempting someone (for example,

Abraham and Isaac in Gen. 22). But the New Testament gives us the fullest understanding of how it works. Satan may tempt us, but while God allows us to be tempted, he does not tempt us himself.

*No evil dooms us hopelessly except the
evil we love, and desire to continue in,
and make no effort to escape from.*

—GEORGE ELIOT

EXAMINE

James 1:14–15 also makes an important distinction between temptation and sin. It is not sin to be tempted to do wrong. It is sinful to act on that temptation, to make a choice for that temptation. Of course, we can make a choice of this sort not only with our minds, but also with our bodies. But this is not a matter of a passing thought. We can't keep thoughts from running through our heads, and it would be foolish to try too hard to stop them. Then we only end up compounding those thoughts. The key is not to let them give birth to choices and intentions. That is when sin is conceived and we are on our way toward death.

EXPLORE

It is human nature to make excuses. Psychologists call it rationalization. We are uncomfortable with the consequences of our actions, so we try to explain them away. These verses reek of the kinds of excuses a person might make excuses like, "The Devil made me do it." Still worse, some might suggest that God was testing them, so it's his fault. But James laid the blame squarely on us, saying that it was our evil desire that led to this sin. We let it seduce us rather than running away. Not only that, but we let it give birth to sin. We are to blame, not someone else, not our circumstances, upbringings, or environments. The blame stops here.

PRAYER

Father, help us to take responsibility for the wrongs we do. Then, as we accept our guilt, may we also accept your forgiveness.

Day 5
OUR TRUE SOURCE
James 1:16–18

INTRODUCTION

God is not the source of temptation. No, he is the source of every good and perfect gift. The gifts that come from him are always good.

ENGAGE

In Malachi 3:6, God firmly proclaimed, "I the LORD do not change." In that instance, God was talking about the fact that he will always take Israel back after they repent. Similarly, James told us that God does not waver back and forth in his desire to give us good things. Yesterday he was the one who gave good gifts. Today he is the one who gives good gifts. And tomorrow he will still be giving good gifts. There is no need to rely on anyone else, and we cannot depend on anyone else to never fail. God is a light that always shines, not a shadow that changes as the sun moves across the sky.

EXAMINE

God gave us birth through the "word of truth," making us a kind of firstfruits of his creation (v. 18). God's word here could involve the Bible, but the background to this statement is probably much broader. Quite possibly, this imagery refers to the seeds of God's will that he has planted in the world. He has given of himself to us and to everyone as the giver of perfect gifts. If we will only let that seed inside us bear fruit, we will be his firstborn children and our lives will bear good fruit. We will be the fruit of God's word in the world. Unlike the conception of evil desires that results in sin and death, God's word in us will give birth to righteousness and life.

EXPLORE

First John wrestles with the person who is born of God and yet whose life yields fruit in hatred and sin. It doesn't work that way, John said (1 John 3:9). In the same way, James thought of the word God has spoken into each of our lives. He has planted a seed in each of us. We are born from that seed. It makes us who we are.

We are part of God's harvest. This great blessing is a gift of God, the great Giver. It is a perfect gift. We should not think that the world has anything better to give us. We should not be deceived so that we are enticed by the gifts it offers, the quick fix, the easy answer.

PRAYER

Spirit, may your seed inside us truly bear fruit for you in the world. Give us the strength to rely on your gifts, not the world's.

BRIDGING JAMES' WORLD AND OURS

The heart of James is a conflict between two worlds and two sets of values. Like Jesus in the Beatitudes, James turned the "common sense" values of the world on their head. The world says, "Go with what you can see, not what you can't." The world says to avoid trials and sufferings as much as you can. The world says, "If it feels good, do it."

But this is not God's world, the unseen world that is breaking in on the world we see. This is a kingdom that the poor in spirit will inherit (Matt. 5:3). This is a kingdom in which the persecuted will reign (Matt. 5:10). It is a kingdom where those who suffer now will prevail then, where those who do not indulge themselves now will be indulged then.

So many Christians do not live on the edge every day. It's easy to forget that God is the giver of all perfect gifts. We can become comfortable and forget we even need God. Our own abundance can make us blind to those who are in need or, worse, make us callous toward them. May the Lord help us live in knowing dependence on him and never have to prove it to us by hardship.

All good things on earth are God's. . . . They are good if we recognize where they came from and if we treat them the way the Designer intended them to be treated.

—Philip Yancey

EXERCISE

For a whole day, try to be aware of every good gift God has given you. Thank God for everything, from the fact that you are alive another day to the fact that you have food to eat and a bed in which to sleep.

Week 2

DOERS OF THE WORD
James 1:19—2:13

Do not merely listen to the word, and so deceive yourselves. Do what it says. . . . But whoever looks intently into the perfect law that gives freedom, and continues in it—not forgetting what they have heard, but doing it—they will be blessed in what they do.

—JAMES 1:22, 25

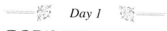

Day 1

GOD'S WORD IN US
James 1:19–21

INTRODUCTION

Many would argue that these verses mark a transition from the opening introduction of the letter to the body of the letter. In the introductory words, James set the tone for the rest of the letter. Here he dug in.

ENGAGE

Emotions are a rich part of being human. They are very powerful motivators both to action and inaction. And anger is one of the strongest. It can be a very powerful motivation to action, but it can also result in great damage to others. Ephesians 4:26 puts it so well: "In your anger do not sin." Anger in itself is not sin, although it is a sin to let anger go on indefinitely, as the rest of Ephesians 4:26

reminds us—don't continue to be angry beyond today. We can feed anger. We can perpetuate anger. This is a path to disaster. Emotions are neither right nor wrong. They just are. It is what we do with them that is right or wrong.

EXAMINE

James already mentioned that God gave new birth to us by planting his word inside us. Here he extended the image. A group of philosophers known as the Stoics spoke of God's word being a seed inside of all of us. With that *logos* (meaning "logic") inside us, we face a choice: Will we accept that implanted word, or will we resist it? Interestingly, the Stoics saw emotions as a key distraction from that logic inside us. There was an obvious choice to make, namely, to submit to the word, which is God's will. Quite possibly, James made this imagery Christian. "Moral filth" (James 1:21) doesn't fit with God's word inside us, nor does succumbing to anger. Rather, we need to act in accordance with God's will for us.

EXPLORE

Some people find it easy to listen to others and be slow to speak. Sometimes such individuals need to speak up a little more often. They are robbing the rest of us of their wisdom and insights! However, just as often, people are too quick to speak. How many parents have jumped to conclusions and wrongly scolded or punished a child? Some of us make this leap when we hear something in the news or on television. If we are interested in the truth, we will listen before we speak. And if we love the quiet people among us, we will silence our voices long enough to let them give their two cents' worth.

*Anybody can become angry—that is easy,
but to be angry with the right person and to the
right degree and at the right time and for the
right purpose, and in the right way—that is not
within everybody's power and is not easy.*

—ARISTOTLE

PRAYER

Spirit, help us see with clarity the choices before us, the choice you want us to make, and the distractions of unhelpful desires.

Day 2

BE WHAT YOU ARE
James 1:22–27

INTRODUCTION

While some think the body of the letter has already begun by this point, others point out that we are still being introduced to themes James fleshed out later, like keeping a tight rein on our tongues.

ENGAGE

In these verses, we hear more themes that will also show up later in the letter. James told his audience to keep a tight rein on their tongues, a theme to which James would powerfully return in chapter 3. His mention of orphans and widows anticipates chapter 2, where James emphasized the importance of putting deeds with our words. Being doers and not merely hearers is a big aspect of that same discussion in James 2. There are benefits to following these instructions—blessing. They will not necessarily be material blessings, but God will honor us for serving him. And James was not pessimistic about us being able to do it. Rather, he *expected* us to be blameless in such things.

EXAMINE

What is the "perfect law that gives freedom" (1:25)? Is it not the same as the royal law that James mentioned in 2:8—"Love your neighbor as yourself"? Love for James was not a feeling. Loving your neighbor had to do with concrete, demonstrable acts of love. He captured this kind of love aptly in 1:27. What does it mean to be authentically religious? It's not about saying religious things (1:26). A much more accurate indicator of true religiousness is helping those most in need, individuals such as orphans and widows. In James' world, there were no social services to take care of these most vulnerable groups. If there was no additional family, such children might be lost to the streets, and such widows abandoned to starvation.

EXPLORE

At some point you may have heard the saying "Become what you are." What are we as Christians? We are the children of God. We are witnesses to Jesus in the world,

God's ambassadors and representatives. We are declared righteous by God. So do we look like it? Do our lives look like we are God's kids? Do we make our Father proud, or are we children who makes others wonder if God is really our Father? Do our lives reflect well on Christ? Do others look at us and think, "I think I'd like to be part of that group"? We know what we are in the mirror. Do we remember it after we walk away and live in the world?

I want to help you to grow as beautiful as God meant you to be when he thought of you first.

—George MacDonald

PRAYER

Father, may others look at us and immediately say, "I know who her Father is," or "He is the spitting image of his Father."

NO FAVORITISM
James 2:1-7

INTRODUCTION

James 2 launches with instruction to Christians everywhere not to show favoritism in worship to people simply because they are wealthy. In church everyone is of equal status, regardless of their status in the world.

ENGAGE

This can be a difficult attitude to play out. In the world, power and money matter. They have immense consequences. In the world, how you dress matters. A first impression is often a lasting impression. In the church, none of that should matter. Obviously, we do not treat the wealthy as *less* important than the poorer in our congregations, but things such as material possessions are trivial in eternity. Well dressed, badly dressed—they are precious in his sight. Able to give, not able to give—Jesus died for both. Successful in business, can't seem to get a break—both are created in the image of God. James made it clear that we must treat everyone with the same love, no matter how wealthy or powerful they are.

EXAMINE

James made an interesting side comment that the rich were the ones who were exploiting Christians, the ones dragging believers into court (2:6–7). He mentioned that they were the ones slandering Jesus' name. Later in the letter he condemned the rich for murdering "the innocent one" (5:6). There is debate over who was murdered here. Did James have Jesus in mind? It would be easy to think of the Jerusalem leadership here. Wealthy priestly families were one element in the leadership of Jerusalem. Prominent rabbis made up another group. Most of these leaders were probably wealthy. Yet most of them seemed hostile to Christians. The high priest not only was a key player in the death of Jesus, but also in the death of James himself.

EXPLORE

Hopefully, few churches today would give special seating to someone just because he or she was rich. Nevertheless, there are many other subtle ways churches may show favoritism to those of greater worldly status than to others. Even our body language can say to some, "You are very welcome here!" and say to others, "I wouldn't care if you never came back." There can be worldly consequences when we do not pay enough attention to those who are powerful and expect favoritism. We have to be shrewd as serpents in such instances (Matt. 10:16). We have to know that such individuals thereby demonstrate that they are not kingdom-minded, yet we also do not want them to hurt the church.

So in Christ Jesus you are all children of God through faith. . . . There is neither Jew nor Gentile, neither slave nor free, nor is there male and female, for you are all one in Christ Jesus.

—GALATIANS 3:26, 28

PRAYER

Jesus, help us to keep in mind that you died for everyone, and that you do not play favorites on the basis of earthly status.

Day 4
THE ROYAL LAW
James 2:8–11

INTRODUCTION

James extended his warnings against favoritism with the underlying reason why it is wrong in the first place. When we show favoritism, we are not loving a "neighbor" who is equally important to God.

ENGAGE

The command to love is not only the central command of the New Testament. It is the ultimate Christian ethic. We are to love God with all our being, and we are to love our neighbor (Matt. 22:34–40). All the expectations God has of us fall into these categories. Indeed, loving one another is the primary way in which we show our love for God. James joined Jesus, Matthew, Mark, Luke,

John, and Paul in passing along this teaching. We are to love one another. Jesus also made it overwhelmingly clear that our neighbor is not merely the people we get along with. Our enemy is also our neighbor. We have to love everybody.

Not only do self-love and love of others go hand in hand, but ultimately they are indistinguishable.
—M. Scott Peck

EXAMINE

The point of James 2:10 is not that the person who kills is guilty of committing adultery, stealing, and the other commands. The point is that you don't get to break one of God's commands just because you keep another one. So, say you are really good at not murdering other people. That does not mean that you are free to commit adultery. And the heart of all the commands is the command to love. If we commit adultery, we have broken the law of love. If we steal, we have broken the law of love. In that sense, when we break any one of God's commands concerning others, we have broken the same law. We have failed to love each other.

EXPLORE

James thoroughly corrected us for thinking we might ignore some of God's expectations because we keep others. Of course James still primarily had favoritism in view, especially the kind of favoritism that ignores those who are in greatest need. The application is straightforward. Whom do we ignore? Whom do we forget is sitting at the table because we are too focused on someone else? Whom do we not see? Do we give our best to one of our children and give the leftovers to the others? Whom do we not invite when we plan things? We do not have to be ministering every moment of every day, but we are all God's ministers every moment of every day.

PRAYER

Jesus, open our eyes to see the people we so often consider invisible.

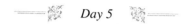

MERCY TRUMPS JUDGMENT
James 2:12–13

INTRODUCTION

These verses finish James' section on favoritism. Here he connected love toward those without power or status to following the law of freedom.

ENGAGE

James' train of thought is a little difficult to follow. He had been talking about the need not to show favoritism to those who are wealthy. It is not enough to follow the law in some areas but not when it comes to loving those in need. Perhaps it is in that context that he spoke of showing mercy. The law that gives freedom (2:12) is presumably the same as the law of love (2:8), which is presumably the same as the perfect law (1:25), which takes care of orphans and widows. Those who have should not look down in judgment on those who do not have. Rather, they should show mercy so that they will also be able to receive mercy from God.

To be a Christian means to forgive the inexcusable because God has forgiven the inexcusable in you.

—C. S. LEWIS

EXAMINE

Christians sometimes debate whether God's justice or God's love is more central to his character. These verses suggest that God's love is the more central of the two. God is eager to trump justice with mercy. This is not the way some talk of God's justice. Some almost treat justice as something to which God is a slave, as if he does not have the authority to set aside justice in the name of mercy. But this is not the sense we get from the New Testament. In the parable of the prodigal son, the father does not have to find someone to pay for his son's sin before the son can be forgiven. God has the authority to forgive whether someone else pays or not.

EXPLORE

"Mercy triumphs over judgment" (James 2:13). The words of this verse immediately remind us of what Jesus said in the Sermon on the Mount: "Blessed are the merciful, for they will be shown mercy" (Matt. 5:7). God doesn't expect us to be perfect, but he does expect us to be merciful. The parable of the unforgiving servant in Matthew 18 makes the point well. God is more than willing to forgive those who wrong him. What he does not tolerate is someone who does not forgive others. Hopefully this is a lesson that we know deeply as Christians. We must forgive others if we have any expectation of God forgiving us. Otherwise, as in the parable, God may recall our every debt to him.

PRAYER

Father, "forgive us our debts, as we also have forgiven our debtors" (Matt. 6:12).

BRIDGING JAMES' WORLD AND OURS

It is so easy for human nature to get distracted from what is important and central by what is easy. It is easy to show favoritism to those who have the power to make our lives easier (or to make them much harder). It is easy to ignore those from whom we stand to gain nothing or, even more possibly, those who might drain us of our time, energy, and resources. It is harder to treat the same those who are insignificant by worldly standards and those who have great power and influence. Loving everyone equally is hard.

It is also much easier to follow a set of absolute rules than it is to wrestle with the hard questions of how love plays itself out in complex situations. It is easier to say, "We must never do that under any circumstances," than to dig in deep, pray hard, and dialog with each other on what the loving thing to do is in each situation. Yet it is to love—not a set of rules—that Christ has called us. To follow is fraught with ambiguity and uncertainty, but it is the path of the kingdom.

EXERCISE

Reflect for a few moments on your key interactions with others today. Now ask yourself these questions: Did I demonstrate love to them? Did I show favoritism? Did I ignore anyone today? Resolve to improve tomorrow if your check-up uncovered any unloving moments.

Week 3

FAITH AND WORKS
James 2:14–26

As the body without the spirit is dead,
so faith without deeds is dead.

—JAMES 2:26

Day 1

DEEDS, NOT WORDS
James 2:14-16

INTRODUCTION

James continued the general theme he had been hammering home since the end of chapter 1. Faith is not just about what you think. What you do is also an essential part.

ENGAGE

James pointed out a fundamental contradiction between those who talk about loving others and those who prove their love by their actions. It is similar to Jesus' parable of the sheep and the goats. Jesus sent a group off to eternal punishment who were surprised at this judgment. Because they did not clothe the naked, feed the sick, or give drink to the thirsty, they were not saved. Similarly,

James said faith that does not demonstrate itself in the concrete love of others is not sufficient to save a person from God's judgment. It is a "no good" faith, in James' estimation. We are our brother's keeper as Christians.

You have not lived today until you have done something for someone who can never repay you.

—JOHN BUNYAN

EXAMINE

Poverty was fairly straightforward in James' day. There were people who needed food and clothing and had no means whatsoever to get it. Family was the primary back-up plan, but an orphan or a widow might not have any. There were no jobs to apply for, no government assistance programs like today. Either someone found it in his or her heart to give you something or you were lost. The situation is a little more complex today. What does it mean to help someone today? Certainly it still means not to let someone starve. But some people need help to find a job. A person can also become unnecessarily dependent on others. Helping calls for great discernment.

EXPLORE

You have probably heard the saying, "Give a man a fish and he will eat for a day; teach a man to fish and he will eat for a lifetime." Certainly a believer will not let someone starve or freeze to death if it is at all within one's power to stop it. But even more important is helping others become self-sufficient so that they do not need help the next time. What is difficult is that some people do not want to fish, the causes of which are complex and do not let us off the hook from helping. To love others means to try to help others concretely in all three ways—immediately, by equipping, and by changing mind-sets.

PRAYER

Jesus, keep us from becoming callous to the needs of others. Make us excellent teachers of "fishing."

Day 2
SHOWING FAITH
James 2:17–19

INTRODUCTION

James drew his conclusion: Faith is alive and well only if it results in the fruit of faith, which is loving action. The other version of "faith" is dead.

ENGAGE

We are a little handicapped in English when we read verses like these because we cannot see that the words *faith* and *believe* are actually related. In English these two words have a completely separate history. But in Greek, the original language of James, these are two forms of the same basic root. In Greek the noun for "faith" or "belief" is *pistis*. Meanwhile, the verb for "believe" or "to have faith" is *pisteuo*. So when the demons "believe" in 2:19, they have faith of a sort. But it is just a "head faith." It is not a "heart faith." They have a faith that is dead, like the person who believes the right things but whose actions do not show it.

*Action speaks louder than words but
not nearly as often.*

—Mark Twain

EXAMINE

The central creed of Judaism is Deuteronomy 6:4: "Hear, O Israel: The Lord our God, the Lord is one." So the majority of Jews believed there was only one true God, and all the believers James addressed—Jewish and Gentile believers alike—believed in only one true God. Still, James pointed out that the demons have that much faith, and they are still pretty scared. By analogy, it is not enough simply to confess the Christian creeds. It is great if someone believes in the Nicene Creed, even several creeds. But it is not enough. We can assume that the demons have a far more detailed and accurate sense of God than any human ever has. It just isn't enough.

EXPLORE

James 2:18 gives the takeaway for this whole section: We should show our faith by our works. It is so easy to say the right words. We can figure out what someone else wants us to say and say it. We can unthinkingly try this tactic with God. We can tell God the right words. But God has already given his sense of such people: "These people come near to me with their mouth and honor me with their lips, but their hearts are far from me" (Isa. 29:13). God is only interested in words that follow through into actions. We show God the faith that makes us right with him in the way we treat others.

PRAYER

Jesus, may the faith that we have in you be nothing like the faith that the demons have. May our faith result in works.

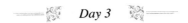

Day 3

ABRAHAM'S EXAMPLE
James 2:20–22

INTRODUCTION

James now gives an example of how faith and works go hand in hand together. The example is that of Abraham, who showed his faith by his obedience.

ENGAGE

James argued that Abraham's faith was not simply Abraham's statement of trust in God—telling God that he trusted him. "Trust" is another possible translation for the word *faith*. Abraham's trust was completed when he went to offer Isaac as a sacrifice. Abraham demonstrated his trust in God. Abraham trusted that God would keep his promise, even though that promise was supposed to come through Isaac. Did Abraham trust that God would find another way? Did Abraham trust that God would raise Isaac from the dead? We cannot know exactly what version of trust in God James had in mind precisely. What we can see is that James believed that Abraham's actions, being obedient to the point of killing Isaac, showed the highest level of faith.

*Life can only be understood backwards;
but it must be lived forwards.*
—SØREN KIERKEGAARD

EXAMINE

A friend and I once built a stairway into an attic we were converting into a room. Knowing that I am a rather bookish person, it was not surprising that some of my family members were a little hesitant to try the stairs once they were done. Yet it did not even occur to others to question the soundness of the structure. They went right up. It may have been appropriate to question my handiwork, but this is a great example of true faith. One person might say, "I have faith in you," but reveal a lack of faith in his hesitancy. Meanwhile, the other person made her faith complete by going up the steps without question. True faith shows itself in what it does.

EXPLORE

Do your faith and your actions work together? If you believe in miracles, do you leave room for God to do unexpected things in your life? James called the person who only cares about what a person believes a foolish person. James called his or her faith useless because it does not do anything. Is our faith useless? Would a non-believer look at us and not be able to see any difference between our actions and those of anyone else? In particular, would our unbelieving neighbor look at our lives and say, "She is more loving than I would expect" or, "He helps others and expects nothing in return"? Does your faith go all the way to completion? Is your faith a "useful" faith?

PRAYER

Father, may we show our trust in you by our eagerness to act it out in a life filled with obedience.

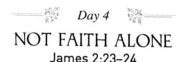

NOT FAITH ALONE
James 2:23-24

INTRODUCTION

In these two verses, James finished his thought about Abraham. Abraham was declared right with God not only because of what he believed with his head, but also by his actions.

ENGAGE

It is hard to read James 2:23 and not conclude that James was in dialog with Paul. Paul quoted the very same verse from Genesis to argue that Abraham was made right with God by *faith*, not works (Rom. 4:3). So did James contradict Paul? I do not believe so, even if James might have thought he did. For Paul, true faith bears fruit, just as James also believed. The "works" that

Paul said did not justify a person were not good works in general but "works of law," that is, especially those parts of the Jewish Law that separated Jew from Gentile. Circumcision, food laws—these were the kinds of things Paul said could not make a person right with God.

EXAMINE

It was this section of James that led Martin Luther to consider it an "epistle of straw." Fixated on his sense that the Roman Catholic Church taught salvation by works, Luther went to the opposite extreme and discouraged thinking about works at all. He added the word *only* to his translation of Romans 3:28, so that it said that a person is made right with God "by faith alone." But Paul did not actually say that—and James explicitly disagreed in 2:23. Indeed, as much as Luther may have liked Ephesians 2:8–9, the next verse goes on to say that God created us for good works. We can quibble over what we are actually saved by, but both *must* be present.

EXPLORE

Most Protestant traditions deal with the faith and works issue by saying that faith is what makes us right with God or "justifies" us. But if faith is true faith, then it will result in a life filled with works. So are works part of the final equation? Matthew 25 seems to say so. James 2 seems to say so. Interestingly, even Paul seemed to have said so. In 2 Corinthians 5:10, Paul said that we will give an account at the final judgment in relation to the works we did when we were in our bodies. The bottom line is that if we truly have God's Spirit inside us, our lives will demonstrate love, joy, peace, forbearance, kindness, goodness, faithfulness, gentleness, and self-control (Gal. 5:22–23).

When you get your "Who am I?" question right, all of your "What should I do?" questions tend to take care of themselves.

—Richard Rohr

PRAYER

Spirit, whether or not we think we have faith and works figured out, fill our lives with these spiritual fruits all the same!

Day 5
LIVING FAITH
James 2:25–26

INTRODUCTION
James finished his line of thought about faith and works with another Old Testament example. This time, it is the example of Rahab and how she hid the spies.

ENGAGE
James 2:26 compares faith and works to a body and a spirit. In James' analogy, faith without works is like a body that does not have a spirit inside it. It is dead, lifeless. That body does not do anything. It is a great analogy. The things we do give life to our faith. We probably should not even call something faith if it is just a head belief. True faith, living faith, involves a confidence in God that changes the way we live. True faith, living faith, results

in faithfulness to God. Faith in Jesus as Lord means that he truly becomes our Lord and thus the Master whom we obey. Anything less is a dead faith.

*You don't have a soul. You are a Soul.
You have a body.*

—C. S. LEWIS

EXAMINE

Rahab is a very interesting choice for an example of how faith needs works in order to be a legitimate faith. Rahab is mentioned only three times in the New Testament, one of which is Jesus' family tree in Matthew 1. Interestingly, Hebrews 11:31 then mentions Rahab as an example of faith. She welcomed the spies even before it was clear that they would be the victors. Although we have to guess at what James was exactly thinking, we can guess that Rahab not only believed that God was on the side of the spies; her actions embodied that faith. She hid them and sent them another way, at great risk to herself. She is thus another great example of what "completed faith" looks like.

EXPLORE

I once talked to someone who knew I had written a book on Hebrews, but he assumed I did not know much about Paul, since I had not written about him. The thing was, I had lots of thoughts about Paul. I had even read a lot about Paul. My point is that we can have a lot of thoughts in our head, but they make no impact on the world if we do not do something with them. My daughter may have great potential to be a tennis player, but I will not call her one unless she plays some tennis. So also, others will know we are children of God when we actually behave like his children in the world.

PRAYER

Spirit, give life to any deadness in our bodies. Strengthen any weak knees of faith or drooping arms. Make our faith come to life.

BRIDGING JAMES' WORLD AND OURS

The verses we have looked at this week challenge us with this question: What should faith look like in our lives? In other words, what would it mean for faith to be "complete" in us?

I may say I believe that God has all power and is in control of the world. Do I then have enough faith to let him take care of things? Or do I feel like I have to take control? Do I feel like if I do not plan, then God will not do anything?

Do I trust God to take care of the wrongdoer? Or do I feel like if I don't catch the person doing wrong, then he or she will get away with it?

It is natural for a human being to get nervous in a dangerous situation is natural as a human being. John Wesley was nervous while sailing to the Americas in the 1700s. But there were others on the ship who did not, because they trusted God.

Of course the "completed faith" that James was most interested in has to do with love. Do I love others in a real and concrete way? If I affirm that "God is love," does my life show it?

EXERCISE

Spend at least twenty minutes in prayer today. Ask God to show you any inconsistencies in your faith. Are there any places in your life where the way you act does not fit with what you say you believe? Change accordingly!

Week 4

TAMING THE TONGUE
James 3:1–18

Who is wise and understanding among you?
Let them show it by their good life, by deeds done in
the humility that comes from wisdom. . . . But the wisdom
that comes from heaven is first of all pure; then
peace-loving, considerate, submissive, full of
mercy and good fruit, impartial and sincere.

—JAMES 3:13, 17

Day 1
TEACHERS BEWARE!
James 3:1–2

INTRODUCTION

James next took up a theme that he mentioned at the end of chapter 1, namely, the need for believers to control their tongues. This is yet another area where faith should show up in action in our lives.

ENGAGE

James addressed those who might teach within the Christian movement. He probably did not have a specific position or office in mind. After all, there are always people to whom others look for guidance and instruction or to help them understand the biblical texts. And there are always people around who think they have something to teach and who seek to instruct others. For example, although we think of Paul as an apostle, it is not at all certain that James did. James might have considered him a teacher, a rabbi of sorts. One dynamic of the early church was traveling teachers. There were good ones, like Apollos, but there were also false teachers, who led people astray.

There is plenty to be learned even from a bad teacher: what not to do, how not to be.

—J. K. ROWLING

EXAMINE

James indicated that no one is perfect: "We all stumble in many ways" (3:2). It is important that he did not use the word *sin* here. When he talked about sin later in 4:17, he had in mind intentional, conscious wrongdoing. Nevertheless, he said what we all know so well—we all fail, especially when it comes to the things we say. James 3:2 is one of the only places in the New Testament where the word *perfect* is used the way we normally use the word in English. In most other cases, it either means "mature" or something like "complete." A mature person still makes mistakes. And a person can go the whole way with God and still fail at some details.

EXPLORE

I have spent two decades of my life teaching, and the words of James 3:1 are always sobering. Anyone who dares to teach others—especially if others listen to him or her—bears the burden of possibly leading them astray. For many years, I taught young college students. At times I was taken aback (even if it was an idea I agreed with) by how quick some of them were to take up a new idea that they were hearing for the first time. "Slow down," I would think. "You should not just take my word for it. Do some investigation. Pray a little about it. Consult others. Don't just take my word for it."

PRAYER

Spirit, give us discernment to test the spirits we encounter in the teaching of others and in our own thoughts. Keep us from going astray.

Day 2

BRIDLING THE HORSE
James 3:3-8

INTRODUCTION

These verses give several examples of large objects, like horses and ships, that can be steered by small objects, like bits and bridles and rudders. So the tongue, even though little, can have a disproportionate impact on others and the world.

ENGAGE

James' examples are taken right from the ordinary lives of his audience. They would have seen horses and how riders are able to steer those horses with a bit and bridle. Living around the Mediterranean Sea, most of them would have seen a ship at some point, and they may have marveled at how one man in the back of a large ship could turn it by himself. Similarly, the tongue is a small part of the body, yet it can have an immense effect on those around us. We can also make "great boasts" (3:5) with it that can get us into big trouble. Clearly it is very important for us to be able to steer it properly!

A knife wound heals, but a tongue wound festers.

—Turkish proverb

EXAMINE

James said that our tongues can set our whole life on fire and that it, in turn, is set on fire by hell. The word he used for hell is *Gehenna*, one of two main words for hell. For example, *hades* is a way of talking about the realm of the dead in general, whether they are righteous or unrighteous. When Matthew 16:18 says that the gates of hell will not prevail against the church, it is talking about the gates of death. But the hell mentioned in James 3:6 is the place prepared for the Devil. Like an arrow lit by a Roman soldier before shooting, the tongue can be lit on fire by Gehenna and in turn set our lives on fire with evil.

EXPLORE

The tongue "is a restless evil, full of deadly poison" (3:8). Most of us at some point have said something we wish we could take back. Sometimes we can almost see the words escaping our mouths into the air. The wrong words at the wrong time can break a marriage just as sure as an affair. In a bad neighborhood, they can get a person killed. They can result in unemployment if we say them to the wrong person. James exclaimed that no one can tame the tongue. With humans it is impossible. But with God, all things are possible. We cannot give up, even though it is so very difficult.

PRAYER

Spirit, tame our tongues. We cannot do it. Only you have the power to steer our lips to speak righteously.

Day 3
A CONSISTENT MOUTH
James 3:9–12

INTRODUCTION

These verses especially fit well with what James had said in the previous chapter. How can we say we love God if we are constantly unloving toward our brothers and sisters in Christ?

ENGAGE

James targeted the person who claims to serve God and yet is hateful toward people. He made some basic observations. Fresh water and salt water do not come out of the same spring. Fig trees do not bear olives. Grapevines do not yield figs. In the same way, how can someone who blesses God turn around and curse those who are an image and reflection of him? Like the person whose works do not fit with the faith he or she claims, so those who curse their neighbors call into question whether their praise of God is sincere. If we love God, we will love others. If we do not love others, it must be because we do not fully love God.

People will forget what you said. People will forget what you did. But people will never forget how you made them feel.

—Maya Angelou

EXAMINE

We should not curse others, because they "have been made in God's likeness" (James 3:9). James did not restrict this comment only to believers. He said we should not curse any other human being, believer or not. Why? Because all human beings are made in the image of God. God created everyone, both male and female, in his image (Gen. 1:27). Christians have long debated what the image of God is. Some say it is our capacity to do good, which Adam lost for us. Some say it includes our ability to reason. Others think it has to do with ruling the creation. But clearly for James it means we are valuable and to be treated with respect.

EXPLORE

It is worth taking a little time to examine whether we say one thing in church and another thing at work and school. Do we bless others with our lips and life, or do we curse them? At church we say, "I love you, Lord," but do we say with our lives, "I hate you, enemy"? To be sure, there are plenty of people in the world who need some correction. If I hate with my tongue, then I am one of them! Am I kind with my words to others? Do I deescalate things by responding softly to a harsh word? Do I build others up or do I tear them down? If I know the right thing to do, I should do it!

PRAYER

Father, purify our tongues from harmful speech to others. May our praise of you make it impossible for us to speak hatefully to others.

Day 4
PROVE IT
James 3:13–16

INTRODUCTION
James 3 started with a warning to teachers. Now in these verses James looked at what true wisdom is really like. It is not about being smart. It is about being loving.

ENGAGE
Paul said we should rejoice with those who rejoice (for example, Rom. 12:15). This is difficult for most of us. It seems more typical for us to be envious when something good happens to someone else. It is not enough for us to have something good happen. Many of us want to be the only one who has something good happen to them. You can see it in young siblings sometimes at Christmas. It is not enough for a child to get a present. He or she has

to have his or her sibling's present as well. Still more, some use their tongues to voice any advantage they think they might have: "Oh yeah? Well, I got *this*!" Such childish behavior is obviously foolish and does not glorify God.

*I would rather be a little nobody than
to be an evil somebody.*

—Abraham Lincoln

EXAMINE

There is a fine line between self-interest and worldly ambition. God created humanity to rule creation and to be fruitful and multiply. What then is the line between doing our best and excelling and the kind of envy and ambition that James warned against? A key difference is that the ambition described in James is the kind that runs over others in order to advance. It is an unloving ambition, and it is ambition described for things that lead us away from God. This is one source of temptation, the tension between our desire to advance and the kinds of things we might have to do in order to advance. We must not succumb to that temptation.

EXPLORE

Socrates noted that true wisdom is more about knowing what you do not know than it is about knowing a lot of things. James 3:13 talks about a humility that comes from true wisdom. How could wisdom lead to humility? True wisdom should lead to humility when we realize God is in fact the one we serve. God's purposes should be the goal of our ambitions. This wisdom puts the world into his perspective and leads to greater order in the world and better lives. Earthly wisdom with its dog-eat-dog rules leads only to greater disorder and evil practices. That wisdom is not from above but is "earthly, unspiritual, demonic" (3:15).

PRAYER

Father, help us catch a glimpse of your greatness so that we will never forget how small we are and how foolish our worldly ambitions are.

Day 5
TEACHING PEACE
James 3:17-18

INTRODUCTION

James 3 ends with a description of what true wisdom looks like. And as it turns out, it is not so much about knowledge as it is about virtue.

ENGAGE

It might be a little surprising to hear finally what the wisdom that comes from above actually looks like. The person with wisdom is peace-loving. A person with God's wisdom is considerate. A person with the wisdom from above is full of mercy, submitted to God, pure, and full of the fruit of the Spirit. The person with wisdom is impartial. This person is truthful and sincere. These are not the typical qualities we think of when we describe wisdom, and they contrast with earthly wisdom, which tries to get ahead by cutting off other people. Earthly wisdom looks to its own advantage, while heavenly wisdom does the loving thing toward others.

EXAMINE

James 3:18 might remind you of Matthew 5:9: "Blessed are the peacemakers, for they will be called children of God." James said that those who sow peace will reap righteousness. This is not the typical human way. We tend to escalate a fight. One person hits and another hits back. The next hit is harder, as is its response. This is how feuds and wars start. It takes heavenly wisdom to defuse situations like these. Peacemaking is an incredibly valuable skill. It takes great inner strength not to strike back, to "turn . . . the other cheek" (Matt. 5:39). Still harder is to get two people to deescalate who are not interested in doing so. Thank the Lord for those to whom he has given this gift.

EXPLORE

It is striking that these verses do not describe wisdom in terms of knowledge at all. Wisdom for James was about virtue. We demonstrate heavenly wisdom by living a virtuous life. This is a sobering thought for those who invest most of their time in relation to what to believe.

As with his discussion of faith and works, James made it clear that God's priorities are not about sorting out ideas but in sorting out lives. And what he wants to sort out is our attitudes toward others. He wants us to be genuine and considerate. He wants us to be merciful and peace-loving. That is what the wisdom from above looks like. Do you have it?

PRAYER

Jesus, make us look more and more like you. Show us your wisdom by making our lives conform to the life you showed us while you were on earth.

BRIDGING JAMES' WORLD AND OURS

Most of us know when we need to control our tongues. Perhaps there are a few people who are so unaware of themselves that the need to talk less and listen more has never occurred to them. It probably will not take long for someone to point it out, hopefully in a loving way.

More difficult is knowing how to tame our tongues. John Wesley had a category of sin that he called "sins of surprise." It referred to moments when we find ourselves doing wrong without giving it a lot of thought. Hurting someone with our words is a good example of that sort of sin. We did not plan to lash out. We did not give it much thought at all. But we did it nonetheless.

How can we stop these sorts of sins? Certainly we can bathe our lives in prayer and think about our words even when we are not talking. With God's help, we can develop the habit of pausing before speaking. If we do it when we are not angry, then we will do it when we are. What we cannot do is nothing. Then we will fail for sure.

*Darkness cannot drive out darkness;
only light can do that. Hate cannot drive
out hate; only love can do that.*

—Martin Luther King, Jr.

EXERCISE

For an entire day, wait at least three seconds before you say something to someone. When a moment is sensitive, wait at least five seconds before responding. How would your relationships be different if you did this every day?

Week 5

GOD'S FRIENDS
James 4:1—5:6

Submit yourselves, then, to God. Resist the devil,
and he will flee from you. . . . Humble yourselves
before the Lord, and he will lift you up.

—JAMES 4:7, 10

Day 1
WRONG MOTIVES
James 4:1-6

INTRODUCTION

James spoke of two kinds of wisdom, one from above and one from below. Here, he spoke of two kinds of friendships. One is friendship with the world; the other is friendship with God.

ENGAGE

Back in James 1, James told believers not to blame God for temptation. Rather, their temptations came from evil desires they had inside. In chapter 4, he explored those desires in a little more detail. Have you ever observed Christians fighting with each other? James linked this arguing to a clash of the selfish desires of one person fighting against the selfish desires of another. The ambitious desires of one clash with the ambitious desires of another. The envy of one urges that person to sabotage the other. It should be obvious that none of these attitudes have any place in the church, even though they are far too common. If we follow the royal law of love, we will not behave in this way.

Do not be yoked together with unbelievers. For what do righteousness and wickedness have in common? Or what fellowship can light have with darkness?

—2 Corinthians 6:14

EXAMINE

James gave an important qualification here on Jesus' teaching in the Sermon on the Mount. In Matthew 7:7, Jesus said, "Ask and it will be given to you." He went on to tell how God our Father wants to give us good gifts (7:9–11). Jesus similarly told his disciples in John 15:16, "Whatever you ask in my name the Father will give you." Yet we know this is not always the case. Sometimes God's answer to our prayers is no. James 4:3 gives us at least one reason why God does not always say yes. It is not the only reason, but God sometimes says no because we ask selfishly. God will not feed our unloving, selfish lusts for things.

EXPLORE

There is some shocking language in these verses, especially 4:4–6. James did not see any middle ground between serving God and loving the world. No, friendship with the world is hatred toward God. James invoked language of God's jealousy from the Old Testament. Those who try to follow both God and human ambition, wealth, or a lust for possessions are committing adultery against God. They are fooling around with a different spouse. James drew on a saying about how God's Spirit inside us becomes jealous in such instances (we do not know the source). We should not be proud of who we are in our worldliness, but we should be humble about who we are before the all-powerful King of the universe.

PRAYER

Father, do not let us trick ourselves into thinking we are something because we have some worldly status or possessions. May we judge our status only in you.

SUBMIT TO GOD
James 4:7–10

INTRODUCTION

Those who have become too friendly with the world are now invited to return to God. It is not too late for them. They can wash themselves and come to God again.

ENGAGE

James did not explicitly use language of repentance, but everything he said fits with a turning of direction from sin toward God. His readers' battle had not just been an inner one, but a fight with spiritual forces as well. They needed to resist the Devil. The Devil had delighted in the fighting and quarreling between believers. He had no doubt taken every opportunity to escalate the conflict. He does not give up simply because we think we have decided to stop our affair with the world. They had been laughing with the world. Instead they needed to turn to mourning. We remember Luke 6:25: "Woe to you who laugh now, for you will mourn and weep." But there is still time.

EXAMINE

So we have turned away from the world and the Devil. What must we do next? We must wash our hands of the affair. We must purify our hearts from their double-mindedness, which we have heard of before in James. In chapter 1, James told us God is eager to give us wisdom in the time of trial, but we must ask, truly wanting to endure the trial. We are now seeing what he was thinking in more detail. We cannot have divided loyalties when we come to God for heavenly wisdom. We must choose God or the world. So we cannot be friends of God unless we purify ourselves of double-mindedness.

EXPLORE

If we have turned away from the world, we must move forward in humility and full submission to God. "Humble yourselves before the Lord, and he will lift you up" (4:10). "Submit yourselves, then, to God. . . . Come near to God and he will come near to you" (vv. 7–8). In these solutions to the problem, we see what the problems were in the first place. The hearts of those who were friends with the world were not near to God. They were near to the world. The hearts of the double-minded were proud of their worldly status and possessions rather than dependent on God. They were trying to be lords of their own lives rather than subjects of the one Lord.

Inappropriate desires regularly produce inappropriate courses of action. If our desires are not kept in submission to God's leading, our pursuits will hardly stay within the boundaries of his commands.

—MATTHEW HENRY (PARAPHRASE)

PRAYER

Father, we submit ourselves entirely to you. Take our hands. Take our feet. Our hearts are yours.

Day 3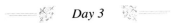

GOD IS THE JUDGE
James 4:11–12

INTRODUCTION

These verses almost seem out of place, but they certainly fit with the underlying theme of loving our neighbors. It is possible that James now turned to those who have been on the wrong end of envy and ambition. God is still the judge.

ENGAGE

It is possible that someone hearing James read aloud in church (that is how these letters made their way into the minds of illiterate Christians everywhere) might have enjoyed hearing others being scolded. Perhaps some of those who were listening had been on the unfortunate side of someone else's ambitions. Perhaps they enjoyed hearing the correction of those who loved the world, while they were suffering. But it is not our place to serve as the final judge. That is God's job. We are also part of God's people because of God's mercy. It is amazing how we can turn things around. We can do wrong when we are actually supporting the right idea. The oppressed can quickly become the oppressor when given the chance.

EXAMINE

We have seen parallels over and over again between James and the teaching of Jesus—especially the Sermon on the Mount. In these verses, we are reminded of another passage. Matthew 7:1–2 says, "Do not judge, or you too will be judged. For in the same way you judge others, you will be judged, and with the measure you use, it will be measured to you." Obviously this instruction does not mean we cannot draw conclusions about right and wrong behavior. Adultery is a sin and it is not judging to say so. However, in other cases we do not know a person's intentions. Even more to the point, it is not our job to make sure a wrongdoer experiences the consequences of his or her wrongdoing.

EXPLORE

Christians should not slander others, whether they have done bad things or not. It is one thing for someone to do wrong, but we compound the problem if we go around talking about them indiscriminately. It is yet another example of how our tongues can get us into trouble. What's worse is that those who slander others often enjoy the problems of others. It makes them feel superior and better about themselves. Clearly such motives are not loving. They advance us at the expense of others. In pointing out where someone else has broken God's law, we break the law ourselves.

*People are almost always better than
their neighbors think they are.*

—George Eliot

PRAYER

Lord, give us the strength to master our tongues when we are tempted to slander others. Sanctify our speech so that it is only pure and uplifting.

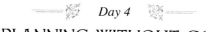

PLANNING WITHOUT GOD
James 4:13-17

INTRODUCTION

This paragraph and the next give James' sternest words toward the wealthy. This one in particular reminds us of Luke's parable of the rich fool (Luke 12:16–20), where a rich man plans for a future he does not have.

ENGAGE

The idea of accumulating wealth in James' day was a little different from today. Most people in the ancient world earned only enough on which to live. Those who expended great energies trying to amass wealth were looked at more like thieves. James considered the plans of a merchant traveling around to make money "arrogant schemes" (James 4:16) that do not make room for God's control over the world. To James, such people did not fully realize that they were just "a mist that appears for a little while and then vanishes" (4:14). This person does not store up treasures for the kingdom of God but invests his or her energies accumulating things for a life that is quickly to end.

Always be in a state of expectancy, and see that you leave room for God to come in as he likes.

—Oswald Chambers

EXAMINE

Couched in James' indictment of the greedy is a window into the nature of sin. Some sins are obvious, like when someone intentionally murders another person. This is called a sin of *commission*. The way James 4:17 is worded makes us think of another important category of sin—sins of *omission*. A sin of omission is when a person does wrong by *not* doing something. We know the good we should do, but we do not do it. Of course, in this case, James was talking about boasting about plans and accomplishments, as if God does not determine the outcome. So the sin in view here is boasting when we know we should be giving God the credit.

EXPLORE

One of my grandfathers was very conscientious about giving God the final decision on whether he would do something. He would say, "Lord willing" whenever he was telling someone what he planned to do in the future—even if it was when he expected to have lunch. Perhaps he was a little extreme, but he certainly modeled what James was saying here. The future is not ours to count on. We are not ultimately in control of what we will be able to do. God is in control. There should always be a little fluidity to our planning because we cannot nail down everything, and it is not our place to nail down everything. That is up to God.

PRAYER

Spirit, may we never be surprised when you change our plans. May they always be conditional on your will.

Day 5
WEALTHY OPPRESSORS
James 5:1–6

INTRODUCTION

The second paragraph on the rich is even more intense. The person in the first paragraph was a merchant who planned without waiting on God. The person in this paragraph is an oppressor, someone who has treated others unjustly even to the point of death.

ENGAGE

As we have seen before, there was general assumption in James' world that a wealthy person was likely unjust. There is an old Arab saying, "Every rich man is either a thief or the son of a thief." It was generally thought at that time that people only became wealthy by taking from others. So James also assumed that the wealthy people he addressed had not paid an appropriate wage to their workers. Laborers had not been able to survive on what the rich had paid them. The rich had become fat while others had starved. They had even brought about the deaths of righteous individuals, and we have already speculated that James may have had Jesus and the leaders of Jerusalem in view.

EXAMINE

James said that the wealth of the rich had rotted and that moths had eaten their clothes. Once again, we are reminded of something Jesus said: "Do not store up for yourselves treasures on earth, where moths and vermin destroy, and where thieves break in and steal" (Matt 6:19). The rich person James addressed had laid up treasures on earth rather than in the coming kingdom of God. This is particularly unfortunate because, as James said, it is the last days. If you knew the end of the world was coming soon and that the Judge was not interested in your money, it would be foolish to devote your energies to acquiring more stuff. Those who do only accumulate more fat for the fire.

EXPLORE

In our world, a person can work hard and make significant amounts of money without cheating anyone or treating anyone unjustly. Accordingly, the economic system of today makes it much more possible for a righteous person to be materially successful. Even John Wesley made significant amounts of money on his books. But he turned around and gave most of it away. Similarly, although Billy Graham could have become rich from his ministry, he only took a modest salary over the years. So while it is not sinful to earn large amounts of money, it does matter what we do with it. In particular, we must pay our employees a salary on which they can live, and God bids us give most of our excess away.

PRAYER

Father, keep our eyes focused on what really matters eternally. Keep them from straying to what we can accrue for ourselves.

BRIDGING JAMES' WORLD AND OURS

I grew up with sermons about not being worldly minded. A lot of that teaching, unfortunately, had to do with things like not wearing jewelry or going to movies. Sometimes it seemed like friendship with the world was reduced to wearing clothes that were too nice or drinking and smoking, like the people in the movies.

I find it fascinating now to look back at how weak this preaching was in comparison to what James had in mind. I do not remember many wealthy individuals in those holiness churches of my youth, but wealth is definitely not something we would hear much warning about today. If anything, capitalism and its benefits have almost become as fundamental to Christianity as the Bible.

The love of the world that James had in mind is a love of material things to the exclusion of loving each other. It is an ambition that ignores other people in order to get ahead. Instead, James wanted us to share all the extra resources God has given us and use them to help others in need. Then we will truly be friends of God.

Earn all you can; save all you can; give all you can.
—JOHN WESLEY

EXERCISE

Pay attention to all the money you spend in one day. Keep track of the total amount of money you spent and what you spent it on. Now calculate how much you would have spent if you only bought what you needed to survive. What is the difference? That is how much you could have given away.

Week 6

THE LORD IS COMING!
James 5:7–20

Be patient, then, brothers and sisters, until the Lord's coming. See how the farmer waits for the land to yield its valuable crop, patiently waiting for the autumn and spring rains. You too, be patient and stand firm, because the Lord's coming is near.

—James 5:7–8

Day 1

BE PATIENT
James 5:7–9

INTRODUCTION

We now begin the closing section of the letter. James shifted to the question of the "meantime." How should the church operate as we wait for the Lord's return?

ENGAGE

These verses remind us a little of the book of Hebrews. James urged Christians everywhere to be patient as they wait for Jesus to return. James did not in any way emphasize this theme, but it must have more and more become an issue as the first century unfolded. James told them to be patient like a farmer who has planted a crop but is waiting for the land to yield the fruit. The farmer not only has to wait for the rains in the fall, but the rains in the spring as well. In the same way, James urged patience of the church as they awaited the final return of Christ.

EXAMINE

You may have noticed that James did not actually mention Jesus very often. Indeed, this is only the third time in the letter that he did (see 1:1; 2:1). It is even possible that he was talking about God the Father here, although he was probably thinking of Jesus. The book of James is much more about ethics—how to live—than it is about Jesus or about theology in general. So these verses are really the first point in the letter where Jesus' return and, by implication, the coming judgment is mentioned. Perhaps it stood in the background of the earlier parts of the letter, but only now does it really come close to the surface.

EXPLORE

When we are waiting for something that we eagerly want or need—and we're not sure when it is going to come—we can get grumpy. We can be irritable. James seemed to have been addressing a church that was grumbling. He reminded them that they wanted to be on their best behavior when Christ returns. They did not want to be fighting when the Judge comes. But this is human nature, is it not? We tend to take out our frustrations about something else on the people around us. A parent who is frustrated with work is more likely to get angry with his or her children than someone for whom everything is going great. We have to watch ourselves to keep this from happening.

*Restlessness and impatience change
nothing except our peace and joy.*
—Elisabeth Elliot

PRAYER

Jesus, give us patience as we wait for your return. Keep us from grumbling in the meantime, as we watch the fields for harvest.

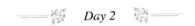

Day 2

PATIENCE IN SUFFERING
James 5:10–12

INTRODUCTION

The previous verses spoke of patience in waiting for the Lord in general. But the suffering of early Christians made the waiting even more difficult. James gave examples of patience in suffering.

ENGAGE

The main example James gave of patience in suffering is Job. God had pointed out to Satan that Job was a person he could not successfully tempt to sin. Satan wagered that he could bring Job to sin if he were to bring calamity on his life. Satan took away Job's wealth, family, then finally his health. But Job did not sin. In the same way, Christians at that time were facing suffering. But James urged them to follow Job's example and patiently wait on justice. In the end, Job was vindicated. In the end, God came and set the record straight. In the same way, James implied, believers should wait on the Lord.

*So comes snow after fire, and even
dragons have their endings.*

—J. R. R. TOLKIEN

EXAMINE

Tucked into this closing section is the curious teaching about not taking oaths. It is not obvious, from our point of view, how this instruction fits into the context, although it may have been obvious at the time. Perhaps those under persecution were sometimes pressured to take oaths of various kinds. But as we have seen repeatedly, James passed on tradition we have heard on the lips of Jesus in Matthew. Jesus said in the Sermon on the Mount not to swear oaths at all (Matt. 5:33–37). We are to be people of truth who do not need to swear. You probably know such people. They are so honest that you believe anything they tell you without question. We are all to be such people.

EXPLORE

In addition to Job, James mentioned the prophets as an example of patience in suffering. So many of them suffered as they spoke God's Word! Hebrews 11 gives a list of faithful witnesses from the Old Testament, many of whom died while being faithful. According to one tradition, Isaiah died by being cut in half. James knew these prophets were held in high respect and admiration by believers everywhere. They were the heroes that Jews looked up to in their history. In the same way, James urged believers to be the heroes of his day, to endure persecution and suffering even if it would mean death. He ended with a reminder of God's compassion and mercy. Suffering will not go on indefinitely.

PRAYER

Spirit, give us the strength to suffer, just as you gave strength to the prophets of old. May we lose ourselves to find ourselves in you.

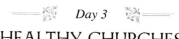

HEALTHY CHURCHES
James 5:13–15

INTRODUCTION

We are to be patient as we wait for the Lord's return. In the meantime, how are we to support each other as communities of faith? How do we bear with each other as we wait?

ENGAGE

We get a beautiful picture of the early church in these verses. Sometimes, communities of faith experienced times of happiness. There were always songs of praise to sing, not only from the Psalms, not only from the Jewish synagogue, but we can also be sure that the earliest Christians wrote songs as well. Some of them may be in the New Testament. There were also troubles to face, just as the book of James says from its beginning. Prayer was always at hand, not only to seek God's help and rescue, but also to pray for the strength to endure. Finally, churches had elders who could pray for people when they were sick, anoint them with oil, and lay hands on them.

Miracles are a retelling in small letters of the very same story which is written across the whole world in letters too large for some of us to see.

—C. S. Lewis

EXAMINE

James implied that there can be a connection between sickness and sin. There is not always a connection, however, as Jesus made clear in John 9:1–3. Sometimes a person is sick from purely natural causes. But James and other passages indicate that sickness can actually be a result of sin. In such cases, it is not just a prayer for health that is needed, but a prayer for forgiveness. Also, in such cases, the anointing of the elders holds great promise for healing. We must always leave room for God to do the unpredictable, according to his will. But God still heals today. Nothing in the Bible suggests he does not.

EXPLORE

There are those in the church today who believe God no longer heals, but James certainly didn't know anything about an expiration date. He wrote instructions to ordinary believers in house churches and told the elders of those congregations to expect healing when they anointed someone who was sick. He was not talking to apostles. He did not warn them that the time was running out on miracles. It is a hope for us even today. To be sure, God does not always heal, and we should be careful not to think that all sickness is sin-related. We should pray for healing, yes. Anointing is always available, yes. But we should seek appropriate medical treatment as well.

PRAYER

Spirit, increase our faith to pray for things that go beyond the ordinary. Make us expectant of the God who created the universe out of nothing.

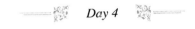

Day 4

THE POWER OF PRAYER
James 5:16–18

INTRODUCTION

James gave the example of Elijah as someone who demonstrated that prayer can change things. So also Christians around the world should have faith that prayer works.

ENGAGE

In the previous section, James encouraged the anointing of those who are sick. In these verses, he encouraged us to confess our sins to one another. We are also to pray for each other, so that our sins may be forgiven and our bodies healed. It is difficult to confess sins to other people, especially when we are truly ashamed of them. It is much easier to tell God in private and let everyone else continue to think we are wonderful. But public confession helps us truly feel the sorrow of wrongdoing, and it also brings accountability to urge us not to fall back into old patterns. God made us to need each other.

Prayer is not asking. Prayer is putting oneself in the hands of God, at his disposition, and listening to his voice in the depth of our hearts.

—Mother Teresa

EXAMINE

If James used Job as an example of patience in suffering, he also used Elijah as an example of confident prayer. It is especially striking when James pointed out that "Elijah was a human being, even as we are" (5:17). We get the message. You cannot say you are not significant enough to move God in prayer like Elijah did. Elijah was a person like you and me. If the faith of Elijah in prayer could move God, then you and I can move God if we pray with confidence. Elijah's prayers took away rain for three and a half years and then brought it back again. Imagine how much we could accomplish for God if we had that much faith!

EXPLORE

"The prayer of a righteous person is powerful and effective" (v. 16). What a powerful verse! How many of us actually feel that way about our prayers? Hopefully we all know some "prayer warriors," people whom we especially ask to pray for us when we are in need. Are we as confident that we can become prayer warriors ourselves? For a long time, 1 Thessalonians 5:17 has stood out to me: "Pray continually." What if I truly sensed that God was always with me throughout the day? I could talk to him all day long as I made my way through the day, driving here and there or sitting at McDonald's for lunch. What would that be if not praying continually?

PRAYER

Father, may our talks together never be like two people who only see each other every once in a while.

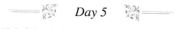
RESCUE THE PERISHING
James 5:19-20

INTRODUCTION

James ended with hope that those who wander from the truth might be brought back. We as believers can play a role in keeping the wanderer from death.

ENGAGE

James' instruction is very practical. Unlike Paul, James did not wax very theoretical. His teaching is very down to earth. So we will not get a lot of theory on the question of whether it is possible to lose your salvation. Some, like me, believe God requires us to be faithful if we expect to be part of his kingdom, no matter how well we start out. Others would say that those who stray were never truly saved in the first place. James did not engage such debates. For him, there are people who wander from the truth and do not make it. We as fellow believers must do all that we can to keep that from happening.

No man is an island, entire and of itself. . . .
Any man's death diminishes me,
because I am involved in mankind.

—JOHN DONNE

EXAMINE

Protestants tend to be very careful about ascribing priestly roles to human beings. Because of Martin Luther's original debates with the Roman Catholic Church, it is very important for us to point to Christ alone as the High Priest who has made our reconciliation with God possible. Jesus is the only *necessary* mediator between God and humanity. At the same time, God uses all sorts of other instruments to draw us close to him, and one of the most significant is each other. God uses people as an instrument to reconcile others to himself (see, for example, 2 Cor. 5:18). These verses in James point to that ministry. It is a ministry that can save someone from death and lead to sins being forgiven.

EXPLORE

It is so easy in American society to worry only about ourselves and our own problems. "No skin off my nose," the saying goes. But this is not the appropriate attitude of a believer toward others. True, some people are meddlers who stick their noses inappropriately into other people's business. That is not the right attitude either. But Jesus bids us to care about the fate of others. Jesus asks us to rescue the perishing, to care for the dying. He uses us as physicians to help administer his healing. One fact we have seen over and over in James is that we *are* our brother's and sister's keeper. Their fate—especially their eternal fate—must matter to us!

PRAYER

Jesus, may we notice those who are in danger like you did. Give us the motivation to reach out to them as you have called us.

BRIDGING JAMES' WORLD AND OURS

The church faces different challenges at different times. The temptations both change and stay the same. There is one set of temptations in a time of persecution and another set of temptations in a time of prosperity. Our sinful nature, egged on by the Devil, will always find ways to express itself if we let it. But at the same time, the Holy Spirit is always present to give us victory over temptation, if we will only let him.

The final section of James is full of the life of the church as it wrestles with challenges from both in- and outside. There is the model of patient endurance that Job showed. Then there is the model of Elijah. God may actually wait on us to decide how to act in the world. We may be the difference between him letting the default play out or intervening to change the course of history.

Then there is the way in which we as believers can intervene in the lives of those in trouble. God has entrusted us with a ministry of reconciliation and the possibility of healing. If we have the faith, he will do more than we could imagine.

EXERCISE

Take a moment to reflect on the community of faith where you worship. Who needs prayer? Who needs a miracle? Very prayerfully, is there anyone who could use rescuing? Pray that the Lord would direct your path.

Historical Reflections on the Early Church

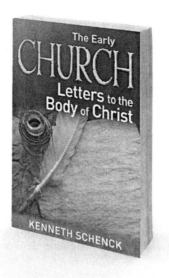

In ***The Early Church—Letters to the Body of Christ***, Kenneth Schenck unpacks the life and world of the early church, revealed through the non-Pauline epistles—those biblical correspondences to churches from Peter, James, Jude, and John—and also through the challenging and rich symbolism of letters written to the Hebrews, as well as John's prophetic Revelation.

The Early Church—Letters to the Body of Christ
978-0-89827-933-7
978-0-89827-934-4 (e-book)

1.800.493.7539   wphstore.com

Deeper Devotions on the Life of Christ

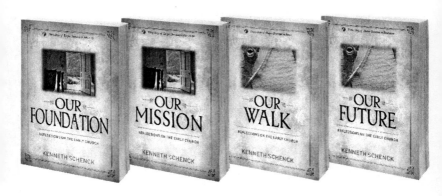

Join New Testament scholar Kenneth Schenck on a journey through thirty days of deeper devotion in these crucial days for Christ's expanding mission. Each devotion will challenge you to engage, examine, and explore the Spirit's work in the church and your life.

Our Foundation
978-0-89827-935-1
978-0-89827-936-8 (e-book)

Our Mission
978-0-89827-937-5
978-0-89827-938-2 (e-book)

Our Walk
978-0-89827-939-9
978-0-89827-940-5 (e-book)

Our Future
978-0-89827-941-2
978-0-89827-942-9 (e-book)

1.800.493.7539　　　wphstore.com

CPSIA information can be obtained
at www.ICGtesting.com
Printed in the USA
FFOW05n0213250915